Oura Ring 4 User Guide

Health and Fitness Tracking, Ring Customization Tips, Sleep Insights, Care and Maintenance for Beginners

By

Paula Todd

CONTENTS

Oura Ring 4

The Oura Ring 4 is not just any smart ring- owning one, is more like having a wellness coach wrapped around your finger. The Oura Ring 4 is designed to be your all-in-one health and fitness companion, tracking everything from your sleep patterns to your body's daily activity, and even picking up subtle changes in your heart rate and body temperature.

Imagine waking up in the morning, and before you even sit up, the Oura app gives you a sleep score, showing how well you slept, how much deep sleep you got, and if you hit that all-important REM stage. It's amazing how much insight it gives into your sleep health, and it's all right there on your phone, ready to help you plan your day.

But that's not all. The Oura Ring 4 has this incredible *Readiness Score* that tells you how prepared your body is for the day's challenges, whether going for a workout, a hike, or just a long day at work. It combines your sleep quality, activity from the day before, and other factors like heart rate variability to give you a personalized "readiness" level. So you'll know if today's the day to push yourself, or maybe take it easy and focus on recovery.

And the activity tracking? Spot-on. It's got you covered with step counts and calorie burns and even tracks the intensity of your workouts. No more guessing if you did enough exercise—Oura's got the data to keep you on track. Plus, it monitors your body temperature and resting heart rate 24/7, which is super helpful for spotting trends in your health.

The Oura Ring 4 isn't just a piece of tech; it's a lifestyle game-changer. It's small, sleek, and fits right in with everyday wear—no need for big, bulky devices. It's like having a health assistant who's always with you, quietly gathering data to help you live healthier and feel your best. If you're ready to take charge of your wellness journey, this little ring is the perfect sidekick.

Why track your health and fitness?

Tracking health and fitness is key to understanding your body and taking control of your well-being. Think of it like having a personal roadmap to better health—it helps you identify patterns, set realistic goals, and make informed decisions that lead to long-term improvements.

Why is it so important?

1. **Building Awareness:** Tracking lets you see where you are right now. You might notice things like restless sleep, inconsistent activity levels, or patterns in your heart rate that you'd otherwise miss. When you see this information clearly, it's much easier to decide what areas to work on.

2. **Setting Goals and Staying Motivated:** When you have a way to measure your progress, it's easier to set achievable goals and see your progress along the way. Whether you're aiming for better sleep, increased daily activity, or a lower resting heart rate, tracking gives you that motivation boost by showing just how far you've come.

3. **Early Health Detection:** Many modern fitness trackers, like the Oura Ring, monitor subtle health indicators like heart rate variability, body temperature, and respiratory rate. These metrics can sometimes flag early signs of health changes, helping you address potential issues before they become bigger problems.

4. **Enhancing Your Workouts and Recovery:** When you track your exercise, you can see what's working and what's not, helping you fine-tune your routines. Plus, monitoring recovery is just as important as tracking workouts. Health trackers show how well your body is resting and recovering, so you'll know if it's a good day to push hard or take it easy.

5. **Better Sleep Quality:** Sleep is one of the biggest factors in overall health, and tracking can help you get the quality rest you need. When you can see detailed information on your sleep patterns, it's easier to make small changes—like adjusting your bedtime or relaxing before sleep—that can make a huge difference in how you feel.

6. **Encouraging Long-Term Habits:** Ultimately, tracking turns healthy choices into regular habits. Seeing daily progress can keep you inspired to make healthy choices each day, building a sustainable lifestyle that leads to lasting wellness.

I must say that tracking health and fitness will help you stay proactive, motivated, and empowered. It's about finding what works best for your unique body and mind, making adjustments along the way, while also building habits that help you live healthier, day by day.

Key features of Oura Ring 4

The Oura Ring 4 offers a powerful suite of health and wellness features packed into a sleek, discreet ring. Key upgrades include a new *Smart Sensing* platform with advanced, asymmetrical sensors that provide more accurate and continuous data, even with slight shifts in the ring's position. Its green and infrared PPG sensors enable 24/7 heart rate tracking, while red and infrared LEDs measure blood oxygen levels during sleep. Additionally, a digital temperature sensor helps detect variations in body temperature, which can provide insight into overall health.

Oura Ring 4 also offers personalized insights into cardiovascular health, tracking metrics like *Cardiovascular Age* and *VO2 Max* to assess aerobic fitness levels. The ring also features *Automatic Activity Detection*, adjusting your daily goals based on your activity levels and stress levels in real-time. A unique *Timeline* feature allows users to log meals and identify patterns, while *Pregnancy Insights* and *Cycle Tracking* provide further personalization for women.

With up to 8 days of battery life and a quick, stylish charging dock, the Oura Ring 4 blends style with functionality, making it a strong choice for those seeking a convenient way to monitor their health closely. The redesigned app organizes metrics into tabs, helping users keep track of daily goals, long-term trends, and stress management easily. This ring is designed not just to monitor but to provide actionable insights to guide healthier living.

Here's a quick summary of these **features**

Smart Sensing Platform – Advanced sensors for continuous, precise health data even if the ring shifts position.

1. **24/7 Heart Rate Tracking** – Monitors heart rate during both activity and rest using green and infrared LEDs.

2. **Blood Oxygen Sensing (SpO2)** – Tracks oxygen levels during sleep with red and infrared LEDs.

3. **Temperature Monitoring** – Digital sensor tracks body temperature variations to identify trends.

4. **Activity and Stress Detection** – Auto-detects activity and adjusts daily goals based on activity and stress.

5. **Cardiovascular Health Insights** – Provides metrics like Cardiovascular Age and VO2 Max.

6. **Pregnancy and Cycle Tracking** – Offers personalized insights for women's health.

7. **Battery Life** – Up to 8 days on a single charge; fast charging dock included.

8. **Enhanced App Interface** – Intuitive tabs for tracking daily goals, long-term trends, and stress.

These features combine to make Oura Ring 4 a powerful, all-in-one health tool.

GETTING STARTED

Let's take a look at what you'll find in the box, as you make a purchase, even as you get your ring ready to start tracking your health.

Your Oura Ring package typically includes the following:

- **Oura Ring** – The ring itself, is available in multiple finishes.

- **Charger** – A compact, stylish dock that charges the ring quickly.

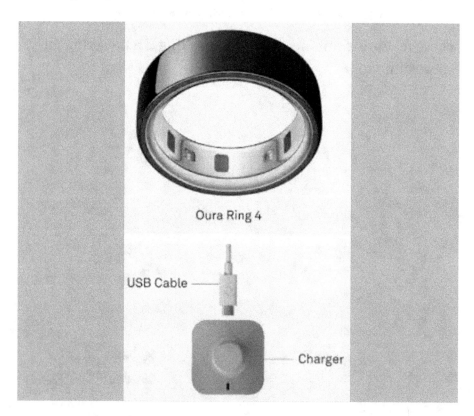

Oura Ring 4

USB Cable

Charger

- A quick guide to help you start with setup and usage tips.

- **Sizing Kit** – Tools to ensure the best fit for accurate readings.

-

How to Charge the Oura Ring

1. Find a stable, flat surface to set up the charger.

2. Plug it into a USB-C port or adapter.

3. **Position the Ring on the Charger** – Place your Oura Ring on the dock with the sensors facing down. A small LED light will indicate charging, which typically completes in 20-80 minutes.

Downloading the Oura App on iOS/Android

1. **Download the Oura App** – Head to the App Store (iOS) or Google Play Store (Android) and download the "Oura" app.

2. **Open the App** – Launch the app and follow the prompts.

3. **Pair Your Oura Ring** – Enable Bluetooth, and the app will guide you through pairing your ring with your device.

Creating an Oura Account

1. **Open the Oura App** – Select "Create an Account" on the app's home screen.

2. **Enter Your Details** – Add your email address, create a password, and fill in other necessary details.

3. **Set Your Preferences** – Customize settings such as notifications, metrics display, and personal goals.

Your Oura Ring is now set up! It's ready to start tracking, analyzing, and helping you optimize your health and wellness.

Pairing the Ring with Your Phone

Now that you've charged it up, it's time to connect it to your phone so you can start tracking your health and fitness.

1. **Ensure Bluetooth is Enabled on Your Phone**

   ○ **iOS:** Go to **Settings** > **Bluetooth** and make sure the toggle is turned on.

   ○ **Android:** Swipe down from the top of the screen to access the Quick Settings panel, then tap the **Bluetooth** icon to turn it on.

2. **Open the Oura App**

   ○ Locate the **Oura** app on your phone and tap to open it. If you haven't downloaded it yet, follow the previous section on downloading and setting up the app.

3. **Start the Pairing Process**

   ○ On the app's home screen, tap **"Add Ring"** or **"Pair New Ring"**.

o   The app will begin searching for your Oura Ring. Make sure your ring is charged and placed on the charger or on a flat surface nearby.

4. **Select Your Ring**

o   Once the app detects your ring, it will display it on the screen. Tap on your ring to select it.

5. **Follow On-Screen Instructions**

o   The app may prompt you to enter a unique pairing code found inside the ring or on the packaging. Enter this code if required.

o   Confirm the connection by tapping **"Pair"** or **"Connect"**.

6. **Finalize the Connection**

o   After a successful pairing, the app will confirm that your Oura Ring is connected. You might see a notification or a confirmation message on the screen.

o   Your ring is now linked to your phone, and data will begin syncing automatically.

7. **Troubleshooting Tips**

If Your Ring Isn't Detected:

•   Ensure Bluetooth is turned on.

•   Make sure your ring is charged and within close proximity to your phone.

- Restart the Oura app and try pairing again.

Still, Having Issues?

- Restart your phone's Bluetooth.

- Turn Bluetooth off and back on.

- If problems persist, refer to the **Troubleshooting** section of your manual guide or contact Oura Support.

Setting up Personal Health Data

To provide you with the most accurate and personalized insights, the Oura Ring needs some basic information about you. Follow this step to set up your personal health data:

1. **Access Your Profile in the Oura App**

   o Open the **Oura** app on your phone.

   o Tap on the **Profile** icon, usually located at the bottom right corner of the screen.

2. **Enter Your Age, Weight, and Height**

   o **Age:** Enter your current age. This helps the app tailor recommendations based on typical health metrics for your age group.

   o **Weight:** Input your current weight. Accurate weight data ensures that calorie burn and activity levels are tracked correctly.

   o **Height:** Enter your height. This measurement is used to calculate your Body Mass Index (BMI) and other health indicators.

To enter or update these details:

- o Tap on **"Personal Information"** or **"Health Data"** within the Profile section.

- o Fill in the fields for **Age**, **Weight**, and **Height**.

- o Tap **"Save"** or **"Confirm"** to store your information.

Set Your Activity Level

- o **Why It Matters:** Your activity level helps the app understand your daily movements and customize activity goals accordingly.

- o **Activity Levels:**

Sedentary: Little to no exercise; mostly sitting or lying down.

Lightly Active: Light exercise or movement a few times a week.

Moderately Active: Regular exercise 3-5 times a week.

Highly Active: Intense exercise almost daily or physically demanding job.

To set your activity level:

In the Profile section, look for "Activity Level" or "Daily Activity".

Select the option that best describes your typical daily activity.

If your activity level changes, you can always update it by revisiting this section.

Additional Personal Settings (Optional but Recommended)

- o **Sleep Preferences:** Indicate your typical bedtime and wake-up time to help the ring track your sleep more accurately.

- o **Goals:** Set specific health and fitness goals, such as increasing daily steps, improving sleep quality, or reducing stress levels.

To set these preferences:

- o Navigate to **"Settings"** within your Profile.

- o Fill in any additional fields like **Sleep Schedule** or **Personal Goals**.

- o Save your changes to ensure the app tailors its insights to your lifestyle.

Review and Confirm Your Data

Double-check all the information you've entered to ensure accuracy. Accurate personal data is crucial for the Oura Ring to provide reliable health and fitness insights.

Sync Your Data

After entering your personal information, the app will automatically sync this data with your Oura Ring. Make sure your ring is close to your phone and connected via Bluetooth to facilitate syncing.

Update Your Information as Needed

As your health and lifestyle evolve, remember to update your personal data in the app. Regular updates ensure that the insights and recommendations remain relevant and accurate.

After these steps, you've successfully paired your Oura Ring with your phone and set up your personal health data. Your Oura Ring 4 is now ready to start providing you with detailed insights.

Choose the Correct Size

Getting the perfect fit for your finger is essential for comfort and accuracy in tracking. Now let us talk about the sizing kit and making adjustments for the best experience.

A **sizing kit** for the Oura Ring is a set of sample rings in various sizes that helps users find the ideal fit before ordering the actual ring. The kit includes multiple plastic rings, each labelled with a different size, allowing you to try on each one to determine which size feels the most comfortable and secure. This ensures that when you receive your actual Oura Ring, it fits well for optimal comfort and accuracy in tracking health metrics.

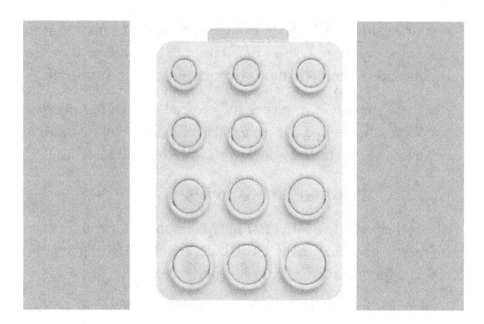

Using the Sizing Kit

1. **Open the Sizing Kit** – Your kit includes a set of sample rings in various sizes. Take a moment to lay them out, and make sure you have adequate lighting.

2. **Try on the Sample Rings** – Each ring size in the kit should be tested on the finger where you'll wear the Oura Ring. Common choices are the index, middle, or ring finger of your non-dominant hand.

3. **Check for a Snug Fit** – The ring should fit snugly but comfortably. It should be easy to put on and take off, without feeling too tight or too loose. Remember, the right fit is crucial, as a secure ring placement ensures accurate sensor readings.

4. **Test During Different Times of the Day** – Finger size can vary slightly throughout the day due to factors like temperature and activity. Wear the sample ring size for a few hours to ensure it remains comfortable.

5. **Choose the Best Size** – After wearing a few options, choose the size that feels the most consistent in comfort and fit throughout the day.

How to Adjust Your Oura Ring for Comfort

1. **Select a Comfortable Finger** – If the fit isn't ideal on one finger, try others. Switching to a different finger can help find the best balance of fit and comfort without compromising on sensor accuracy.

2. **Monitor for Swelling or Temperature Effects** – Rings can feel tighter during hot weather or after physical activity due to slight swelling. If this happens, you may want to try the next larger size in the kit.

3. **Use Ring Adjusters if Needed** – If you find that your finger size fluctuates significantly, consider using a small ring adjuster (a thin, silicone strip) to help your ring maintain a snug fit without causing discomfort.

4. **Wear consistently on the Same Finger** – Once you've found the perfect fit, wear the Oura Ring on the same finger for consistent data tracking. Switching fingers or wearing the ring loosely may reduce tracking accuracy.

UNDERSTANDING THE OURA RING 4 DASHBOARD

The Oura Ring 4 Dashboard in the Oura app is your go-to space for tracking, understanding, and interpreting your health and wellness data. Let's take a closer look at the app's interface and learn how to navigate the key sections.

Interface Overview

Upon opening the Oura app, you'll see a clean, intuitive layout organized into several key tabs, each focused on different aspects of your health:

1. **Home** – This is your main dashboard and provides a summary of your daily metrics, including steps, sleep quality, activity score, and readiness score. It's a quick snapshot of your overall health.

2. **Sleep** – This tab shows detailed insights into your sleep patterns. You'll find data on sleep duration, stages (deep, light, REM), sleep efficiency, and restfulness. The Sleep Score gives you a daily rating of your overall sleep quality.

3. **Activity** – Here, you can view your physical activity throughout the day. The app tracks steps, calories burned, and active time. You'll also see an Activity Goal that adapts based on your recent activity and readiness scores.

4. **Readiness** – The Readiness tab assesses how prepared your body is for physical activity or recovery. This score is calculated based on metrics like heart rate variability (HRV), body temperature, and previous activity levels.

5. **Insights** – This tab provides personalized insights and trends over time, helping you make connections between your daily habits and long-term health. You may also receive tips on improving sleep, activity, or overall wellness based on your data.

How to Navigate the App

- **Tap Each Tab**: Simply tap on any of the tabs (Home, Sleep, Activity, Readiness, Insights) to go into that specific area. Each tab contains more detailed information, charts, and trends related to your daily, weekly, or monthly data.

- **View Daily Summaries**: In each tab, you can see a summary of the day's data. For example, in the Sleep tab, you'll see an overview of your most recent sleep session.

- **Explore Trends**: For more detailed information, look for options to view trends over time, which will help you understand patterns in your health and lifestyle.

- **Access Personal Insights**: The Insights tab will provide you with personalized recommendations, such as reminders to rest or tips for improving your routine based on your trends.

Syncing the App with the Oura Ring

1. **Enable Bluetooth** – Ensure Bluetooth is on for seamless syncing between your ring and app.

2. **Automatic Syncing** – The Oura Ring typically syncs with the app automatically throughout the day as long as Bluetooth is enabled and the ring is near your phone.

3. **Manual Syncing** – If data hasn't been updated, you can manually sync by opening the app and selecting the refresh icon or "Sync Now" button.

4. **Troubleshooting Syncing Issues** – If syncing doesn't occur, try restarting Bluetooth, checking the app's permissions, or even restarting your phone to reset the connection.

By understanding these key sections and keeping your app synced, you'll maximize the benefits of your Oura Ring 4, using the app to guide healthier decisions daily.

Oura Ring Basics

The Oura Ring 4 is packed with cutting-edge sensors that work together to track various aspects of your health, including sleep, activity, and readiness. Here's a closer look at the sensors inside the ring and how they collect your data.

Ring Sensor Overview

1. **Infrared Photoplethysmography (PPG) Sensors**

These sensors use infrared light to measure blood volume pulse from the arteries in your finger. By detecting slight changes in blood flow, they can monitor heart rate, heart rate variability (HRV), and blood oxygen levels.

Unlike visible light sensors, infrared light allows the ring to take measurements without needing bright LEDs, making it more comfortable for nighttime use.

2. **Accelerometer**:

This sensor detects your movement, including steps, intensity of activity, and total time spent moving. It's a critical component for tracking daily activities and estimating calories burned.

The accelerometer also helps measure rest periods versus active moments, which contributes to overall activity and readiness scores.

3. **Gyroscope**:

Working with the accelerometer, the gyroscope measures orientation and angular motion, which provides even more detail on your movements. This allows the Oura Ring to distinguish between different types of activities and to better assess sleep positions, such as lying down versus sitting.

How the Ring Collects Data

- **Sleep Tracking**:

The Oura Ring uses its infrared PPG sensors to monitor your heart rate and HRV throughout the night, while the accelerometer and gyroscope detect your body movements. By combining this data, it can assess sleep stages—light, deep, and REM—and determine sleep efficiency, latency, and overall sleep quality.

- **Activity Tracking**:

During the day, the ring's accelerometer and gyroscope track your steps, calories burned, and movement patterns. It distinguishes low, moderate, and high-intensity activities, adapting your daily activity goals based on previous activity levels to help you maintain balanced energy and recovery cycles.

- **Readiness Tracking**:

The readiness score is a composite measure of your body's capacity for activity or need for rest. It's based on nighttime heart rate, HRV, body temperature variations, and past activity levels. The ring's sensors gather this data while you sleep, providing a readiness score each morning that can guide your exercise intensity or rest needs.

HEALTH TRACKING FEATURES

Sleep Tracking

The Oura Ring 4 excels at monitoring sleep patterns and providing insights that can help you improve rest and recovery. Let's break down how it tracks sleep, how you can interpret your sleep data in the Oura app, and what you can do to improve your sleep score.

How Oura Ring Tracks Sleep Stages

With its infrared photoplethysmography (PPG) sensor, accelerometer, and gyroscope, the ring monitors your sleep across three stages: **light, deep, and REM sleep**.

Light Sleep: This stage is a transition phase where your body is preparing for deeper sleep. The ring tracks periods of light sleep to help provide a balanced view of your total rest.

Deep Sleep: In deep sleep, your body undergoes physical recovery, muscle growth, and immune system strengthening. The Oura Ring uses heart rate data and minimal body movement as indicators of this restorative phase.

REM Sleep: This is the stage associated with dreaming and memory processing. The ring can detect REM by measuring low levels of movement paired with moderate heart rate activity, differentiating it from other sleep stages.

By analyzing these stages, Oura creates a comprehensive sleep profile each night to assess overall sleep quality.

How to Read Sleep Data in the App

1. **Open the Sleep Tab**:

   o Start by tapping on the "Sleep" tab in the Oura app. This is where all of your nightly sleep data is displayed, broken down by different stages and metrics.

2. **View Your Sleep Score**:

   o The app calculates a **Sleep Score** based on factors such as total sleep duration, sleep efficiency, timing, restfulness, and the balance of sleep stages. Scores typically range from 0 to 100, with higher scores indicating better sleep quality.

3. **Explore Detailed Sleep Stages**:

   o Scroll down to see a breakdown of the different sleep stages (light, deep, REM) across the night. A timeline or graph shows when each stage occurred, allowing you to see how long you spent in each phase.

4. **Check Heart Rate and HRV**:

   o The app also displays metrics like **heart rate** and **heart rate variability (HRV)** trends, which give insights into how well your body is recovering. For example, a gradual decrease in heart rate overnight usually indicates a restful sleep.

5. **Review Sleep Efficiency**:

- Sleep efficiency is the percentage of time spent asleep after going to bed. High efficiency (over 85%) means you're sleeping consistently without frequent awakenings.

6. **Monitor Other Factors**:

- The app includes metrics on **sleep latency** (how quickly you fall asleep), restfulness, and wakefulness to provide a full picture of your sleep cycle.

Understand Sleep Score and How to Improve It

The **Sleep Score** is a cumulative metric that provides an easy-to-understand number summarizing your sleep quality. Here's what contributes to it and tips for improving your score:

- **Sleep Duration**: Aim for the recommended 7-9 hours per night to support recovery. Consistent bedtime routines can help achieve this.

- **Sleep Efficiency**: Limiting caffeine and electronics before bed can reduce nighttime awakenings, increasing efficiency.

- **Sleep Timing**: A regular sleep schedule helps your body align with its natural circadian rhythm, improving overall sleep quality.

- **Sleep Balance**: Spend enough time in each sleep stage. Relaxation techniques before bed may help increase time in restorative deep and REM sleep.

- **Restfulness**: To stay restful, avoid heavy meals, intense workouts, or caffeine in the hours leading up to bedtime.

If you pay attention to these factors and make gradual adjustments, you can improve your sleep score. It contributes to better energy, mood, and overall health.

Sleep Insights

The Oura Ring 4 provides personalized insights that will help you understand your sleep patterns, so you can make adjustments for better rest.

Optimal Bedtime

The Ring uses your sleep data, along with insights about your activity, readiness, and past sleep patterns, to suggest an **optimal bedtime**. This recommendation helps you align your sleep schedule with your body's natural circadian rhythm, which is key to waking up feeling refreshed and energized. By analyzing factors such as:

- **Sleep latency** (how long it takes you to fall asleep)
- **Sleep stages** (light, deep, REM)
- **Recovery needs**

Oura suggests the best time to go to bed for the highest quality sleep, thereby helping you achieve a balance between deep and REM sleep. This is important for physical recovery, memory consolidation, and overall well-being.

Sleep Consistency

Maintaining **consistent sleep times** is one of the best ways to improve your sleep quality. Oura emphasizes the importance of going to bed and waking up at roughly the same time each day. Consistency supports the body's internal clock and helps you fall asleep more easily, stay asleep longer, and wake up feeling more refreshed. The app tracks your sleep habits and trends, providing a visual representation of how regular your sleep schedule is.

If there are irregularities, such as frequent variations in sleep times, the app will alert you to make adjustments for better consistency. In turn, improving consistency will enhance your **sleep efficiency** and **readiness scores**.

Viewing Nightly Sleep Reports and Trends

1. **Nightly Sleep Reports**:

After each night's sleep, Oura generates a detailed **sleep report** that includes data on your sleep stages, duration, and quality. This includes a breakdown of **deep sleep**, **light sleep**, and **REM sleep**, along with other vital metrics like **heart rate** and **restfulness**.

The **Sleep Score** at the top of the report provides an at-a-glance view of how well you slept, helping you quickly understand your sleep quality.

2. **Sleep Trends**:

The **Trends** tab within the app allows you to track your sleep patterns over time. By viewing **weekly and monthly trends**, you can spot changes in your sleep habits, such as improvements or setbacks in sleep quality, duration, and consistency.

These trends help you identify what might be affecting your sleep—like changes in activity level, stress, or diet—and provide actionable insights for improving future sleep.

3. **Visual Data Representation**:

The Oura app displays data in easy-to-read charts and graphs, showing how your sleep has evolved over days, weeks, or months. This visual data helps you see if you're on track with your sleep goals and where adjustments might be needed for optimal recovery.

Learn to regularly review these reports and trends, so you can make more informed decisions about your daily habits and sleep environment.

Activity Tracking

Daily activity goals

Oura Ring 4 offers a robust approach to tracking fitness with a focus on heart rate, intensity, and recovery. Here's how it tracks and helps optimize your workouts:

1. **Tracking Intensity & Duration**: The Oura Ring tracks the intensity and duration of your workouts with features like the "Workout Heart Rate" (HR) tracker. It monitors your heart rate during physical activities like running, walking, or cycling, providing insights into your performance by showing average, maximum, and minimum heart rate throughout your workout. You can also view a graph of your heart rate throughout the session, helping you understand your effort and pacing.

2. **Activity Contributors**: The Oura Ring's Activity Score is influenced by several key factors:

Training Frequency: Oura tracks how often you engage in medium to high-intensity workouts. Ideally, you should aim for 3–4 sessions per week to maintain cardiovascular fitness.

Training Volume: It tracks how much medium to high-intensity activity you get over a week. To maintain an optimal Activity Score, Oura recommends achieving around 2,000 MET minutes per week.

Recovery Time: With emphasis on rest and recovery, the ring tracks your recovery time, advising you to have 1–2 easy days each week to avoid overtraining.

These combined features provide a comprehensive view of your activity levels, helping you balance your workouts with sufficient recovery to enhance overall well-being.

Viewing Activity Data in the Oura App

To access your activity data in the Oura app, follow these steps:

1. Launch the app on your phone and head to the **Home tab**.

2. **Select the "Activity" Tab**: This tab shows your daily activity data, such as **steps taken, calories burned, active time**, and movement intensity. Each of these metrics gives you insights into how active you've been throughout the day.

3. **Tap to Explore Specific Metrics**: By selecting any of these sections, you'll get a deeper dive into your daily progress, including suggestions on how to reach your goals and maintain an optimal activity balance.

Customizing Activity Goals

To set or adjust your activity goals:

1. Go to the **Activity card** in the Home tab.

2. Tap **Edit Activity Goal** and use the slider to set a new target that reflects your fitness objectives.

3. Choose whether you want your goals to track **steps** or **calories burned**—this gives you the flexibility to set goals based on your unique preferences and lifestyle.

Heart Rate Monitoring

The Oura Ring 4 delivers continuous heart rate monitoring, tracking your heart rate during the day and night. This is done using already mentioned photoplethysmography sensors, which shine light onto the skin and measure the light reflected back, a method that can indicate blood flow changes tied to heart rate.

Viewing Heart Rate Trends and Insights

In the Oura app, you can view your heart rate data in real-time or check past trends. The **"Live Heart Rate"** feature, accessed from the app's heart rate section, gives you an immediate reading when you hold still for about 10 seconds. The app also provides a **24-hour heart rate graph**, showcasing how your heart rate fluctuates over the day, and highlights periods of activity, rest, and sleep for easy insights into your body's responses to different conditions.

Additionally, Oura tracks heart rate variability (HRV), which reflects how well your body manages stress and recovery, serving as a valuable metric for assessing cardiovascular and general health.

Using Heart Rate Variability for Fitness and Recovery

With this important metric, Oura ring tracks, and particularly helps you understand recovery and stress management. HRV measures the small variations in time between heartbeats, which can indicate how well your body recovers from physical or mental stress. Higher HRV generally suggests a more resilient cardiovascular system, while lower HRV may indicate stress or a need for rest. The Oura app integrates HRV data to provide **Readiness Score insights**, helping you decide when to take it easy and when you're primed for higher-intensity activities.

Body Temperature Tracking

The Ring uses a highly sensitive Negative Temperature Coefficient (NTC) sensor to detect subtle body temperature fluctuations from the skin on your finger. This approach focuses on skin temperature rather than core temperature, which is useful for tracking trends over time, like fever onset, menstrual cycles, and sleep-related temperature shifts. Since the sensor measures temperature changes as small as 0.1°C, the data can help identify shifts that may indicate recovery needs, stress levels, or overall health adjustments.

Oura interprets your temperature in relation to your baseline, not as an absolute number, so it reports deviations (like "+0.2°C") instead of direct readings (like 37°C). This relative measure provides insights without needing precise, lab-level measurements, offering a practical method for wearable tech users to monitor temperature patterns that affect health and wellness. This skin-based measurement approach also allows continuous nighttime tracking without disrupting the user's comfort or routine.

MORE ON FITNESS TRACKING

Tracking Workouts and Exercise

The Oura Ring 4 offers extensive fitness tracking tools to help you monitor various workouts, including the ability to manually log exercises for a tailored fitness experience. You can track specific workouts such as running, cycling, and swimming by selecting them in the app. Additionally, the ring includes a Workout Heart Rate (HR) feature, which tracks average, maximum, and minimum heart rates during each session. This insight helps you assess exertion levels and adapt your training intensity to achieve balanced performance and recovery.

The ring also detects workout duration, distance, and even heart rate zones, which are automatically generated to reflect intensity. You can use this data to gauge exertion levels and ensure that you're staying within optimal ranges for your fitness goals.

How to manually log workouts

To manually log a workout on the Oura Ring app, follow these step-by-step instructions:

1. **Open the Oura App**: Start by opening the Oura app on your smartphone.

2. **Navigate to the Home Tab**: From the main dashboard, go to the "Home" tab, where you can view daily insights and summaries.

3. **Tap on the "+" (Add) Icon**: Look for the plus symbol on the screen, usually located near the top or bottom of

the app, depending on the interface version. Tap this to start logging an activity.

4. **Select "Log Activity"**: A menu will pop up with options like "Log Activity" or similar. Choose this option to start entering workout details.

5. **Choose Activity Type**: Scroll through the list of available workout types and select the one that best describes your activity (e.g., running, cycling, swimming).

6. **Enter Workout Details**: You'll be prompted to input details like the **start time**, **duration**, and **intensity level** (easy, moderate, or hard). Adjust these as needed to reflect your workout.

7. **Save the Activity**: Once all details are entered, confirm and save the activity. This will add to your daily metrics and contribute to your activity and readiness scores.

By following these steps, you can ensure that the Oura Ring reflects your physical efforts accurately, even for activities the ring may not automatically detect. This manual entry can enhance the accuracy of your readiness score and other insights.

.

Use Oura Ring for specific exercises.

To use your Oura Ring for tracking specific exercises, such as running, cycling, and swimming, here's a step-by-step guide:

1. **Open the Oura App**: Launch the Oura app on your smartphone.

2. **Navigate to Activity Tracking**: Go to the activity tracking section in the app, where you'll find options to view and log different activities. While Oura can automatically detect some activities, manual logging is available if you want more precise control.

3. **Start Logging**: If your workout is not automatically detected, manually log it by selecting the exercise type (like running, cycling, or swimming). You can input details such as intensity and duration to improve tracking accuracy.

4. **Automatic Activity Detection**: For many types of physical activities, Oura's Automatic Activity Detection (AAD) will log activity automatically, including metrics such as average heart rate and intensity levels in heart rate zones. For high-energy workouts, Oura uses the accelerometer and gyroscope to detect movement patterns unique to each exercise.

5. **Review Insights**: Once you've completed the exercise, the app displays metrics like heart rate trends, calories burned, and time spent in various heart rate zones. This helps you gauge the workout's intensity and the impact on your fitness.

This approach enables you to view each workout's specific data and adjust your goals over time.

Understand workout recovery scores.

To understand your workout recovery scores with the Oura Ring, you can assess how your body responds to recent activity and its readiness for more. This score combines factors like heart rate variability (HRV), resting heart rate (RHR), body temperature, and sleep data. As you now know - a high recovery score indicates that your body is well-prepared for exercise, while a lower score suggests a need for rest or lighter activity.

Here's how to view your recovery scores:

1. Go to the main dashboard and locate the Readiness Score section.

2. **Access Recovery Details**: Tap on the Readiness Score for a breakdown, where you can view data like your HRV and RHR during the last sleep cycle.

3. **Interpret Key Metrics**: Review factors such as your "Activity Balance" and "HRV Balance," which compare recent physical stress with your long-term averages.

4. **Use Recovery Tips**: Based on your score, the app may suggest adjustments in activity, rest, and even ideal sleep times to help you recover optimally.

Monitor exertion levels during exercise.

To monitor exertion levels during exercise with the Oura Ring, you can use features like heart rate monitoring and activity tracking.

Live Heart Rate Monitoring: use your heart rate in real-time during exercises, such as running or cycling. To measure your heart rate during a workout:

- Open the Oura app and navigate to the "Activity" section.

- Tap on the "Live Heart Rate" feature, ensuring your ring is properly synced and that you remain still for an accurate reading.

- Oura will display your heart rate in beats per minute (BPM) during exercise.

Activity Score: With an "Activity Score" based on the intensity and duration of your workouts, a higher score reflects better activity levels, as aligned with your fitness goals. This helps you monitor if your exertion levels are within optimal fitness zones.

Tracking Exercise Intensity: For specific exercises like running or cycling, Oura uses data from its accelerometer and heart rate sensors to gauge intensity. This data helps assess your exertion levels. This will allow you to adjust your workout accordingly.

How Oura Ring tracks recovery status

The Ring tracks your recovery status by integrating data from various sources, including activity levels, sleep quality, and heart rate. View and interpret your recovery data by:

1. **Open the Oura App**: Navigate to the "Readiness" tab on the home screen. This section provides an overview of your recovery score, which is influenced by factors like

sleep quality, activity level, and heart rate variability (HRV).

2. **View Recovery Score**: The score is colour-coded and reflects your body's current readiness to perform activities. Again, a higher score indicates better recovery, while a lower score suggests the need for rest.

3. **Review Sleep Data**: Oura uses sleep data to assess recovery. Sleep stages, particularly deep sleep, play a significant role in recovery. Ensure you have adequate deep sleep for better recovery.

4. **Check Activity Levels**: Activity impact on recovery is shown in the Readiness tab. Consistent activity that aligns with your fitness level contributes positively to recovery, while excessive strain can lead to lower recovery scores.

5. **Heart Rate Variability (HRV)**: HRV is a key indicator of recovery. Higher HRV suggests that your autonomic nervous system is in balance and recovering well. You can also monitor this in the Oura app under the "Readiness" or "Heart Rate" sections.

6. **Restorative Time**: This feature tracks the periods during your day when your body is in a restful state, contributing to recovery. It's displayed on your 24-hour heart rate graph.

Tips for Improvement: If your recovery score is low, consider improving sleep quality, managing stress levels, and adjusting physical activity. Lower-intensity activities and ensuring proper rest can help improve future recovery scores.

Progress Tracking and Goal Setting

To set fitness goals in the Oura app, follow these simple steps:

1. Launch the app and ensure that your Oura Ring is synced with it.

2. **Access the 'Activity' Section**: Tap on the "Activity" tab in the app's main dashboard.

3. **Go to 'Personalized Goals'**: Under this area, you can review your existing goals or set new ones. Oura automatically suggests a personalized goal based on your Readiness Score, which is influenced by factors like your age, weight, height, sleep, and activity levels.

4. **Adjust Goal Type**: You can choose whether you want your goal to focus on steps or calorie burn. The app will also give you the option to adjust the intensity or duration of your activity goals.

5. **Set or Modify Daily Targets**: If you want to change your goals, you can manually adjust them depending on what's most important to you, such as the number of steps or calories burned.

6. **Review Progress**: As you move through the day, Oura will update your progress towards meeting your goal, allowing you to track your activity levels.

Additionally, Oura offers a helpful guide to improve your Activity Score by monitoring factors like inactivity, training frequency, and recovery time. If needed, you can use the **Rest Mode** feature to mute your activity goals temporarily when recovering from illness or injury.

Understanding Oura's motivation and recommendations

You can leverage the Oura app's insights for improving your fitness, it offers personalized recommendations based on your daily health data, which you can access through the "Today," "Vitals," and "My Health" tabs in the app. Here's what to do:

1. **Accessing Daily Insights**:

Today Tab: This is your central hub where you'll see your daily readiness, sleep, and activity scores at the top. The app dynamically updates throughout the day with relevant insights, such as sleep quality or activity progress, depending on how your day unfolds. If you need to catch up on steps, for example, it will highlight that.

2. **Getting Motivational Feedback**:

In the **Today Tab**, Oura highlights trends or any concerns, such as sleep disruptions or low activity, to help you make adjustments. For instance, in the morning, it may prompt you to focus on rest if your readiness score is low.

The app also shows personalized "Discoveries" based on your tagged habits and how they correlate with changes in your health, offering actionable insights.

3. **Using Data for Long-Term Health**:

Vitals Tab: For deeper insights, the Vitals tab displays your core health metrics (e.g., heart rate, stress, sleep) in chart form, showing how they change over time. It helps you understand which factors, like rest or physical activity, are influencing your scores. This allows you to make informed decisions for sustained health.

4. **Reviewing Longer-Term Trends**:

My Health Tab: Here, you can see a broader view of your progress, including long-term trends like cardiovascular age or sleep consistency, which can guide you in setting future goals and adjustments.

5. **Goal Setting and Adjustments**:

Based on the app's insights, you can customize goals for activity or recovery. For example, if you consistently see low readiness scores, you might aim for more balanced sleep or adjust your daily exertion.

ADVANCED FEATURES

The Oura Ring's **Readiness Score** is a personalized, dynamic metric designed to give you insights into your body's readiness to face challenges, whether physical or mental. It combines several factors to generate a score between 0 and 100. Each score indicates whether your body is prepared for exertion, or not and suggests when rest and recovery are needed.

Calculate Readiness Score

Here's a breakdown of how the Readiness Score is calculated and used:

1. **Sleep**: The quantity and quality of sleep are key contributors to the score. Factors like total sleep duration, sleep consistency, and recovery time after the lowest resting heart rate are assessed.

2. **Activity**: Your activity levels, based on the previous day's movements and the balance of intense or light activity, affect your score. Too little activity or excessive strain can reduce the score.

3. **Heart Rate Variability**: A higher HRV typically suggests good recovery, while a low HRV indicates that your body might be under stress.

4. **Body Temperature**: Fluctuations in your body temperature, especially at night, are tracked. Significant deviations from your normal baseline temperature can

negatively impact your Readiness Score, indicating possible stress or illness.

Interpreting the Readiness Score

To do this:

1. **Open the Oura app** and navigate to the **Readiness** tab.

2. **Check your score**: It will fall between 0 and 100, with scores above 85 indicating ideal readiness, while scores below 70 suggest a need for rest.

3. **Review contributor insights**: The app will break down how each factor (sleep, activity, HRV, etc.) contributed to your score.

4. **Use insights for decisions**: If your score is low, focus on rest and recovery (e.g., sleep, hydration, relaxation). If it's high, consider pushing yourself further in your workouts or taking on a new challenge.

Mindfulness and Stress Management

The Oura Ring helps monitor mindfulness and stress through several features already mentioned, designed to track your body's responses to various stressors and recovery activities. Here's how it works.

Mindfulness Tracking: The Ring doesn't specifically track mindfulness practices, but it provides insights into your physiological state through metrics like heart rate variability

(HRV) and daytime stress. Monitoring your HRV can help you understand your body's adaptation to stress and recovery, guiding you to practices that improve your mindfulness and relaxation. HRV typically rises when your body is in a relaxed state, signalling good stress management.

Stress Monitoring: The Ring's "Daytime Stress" feature, which tracks your physiological responses to stressors throughout the day, analyzes factors like heart rate, HRV, movement, and temperature. This data is then used to categorize your stress level into four zones: **Stressed**, **Engaged**, **Relaxed**, and **Restored**. This gives you a real-time understanding of how your body is responding to internal or external stress.

Viewing Stress Management Insights: This includes real-time stress graphs, showing how your stress levels fluctuate during the day based on your activities. The app also allows you to add tags to identify potential stressors, such as work or social events. By reviewing this data, you can gain insights into what triggers stress and how effectively you recover from it.

Breathing Exercises: Oura integrates breathing exercises with your overall health tracking. While the app itself doesn't lead mindfulness practices directly, its data can help guide you in timing mindfulness activities, such as deep breathing or meditation, to manage stress effectively. You can incorporate these activities into your daily routine, especially when the app shows low recovery or high stress.

BATTERY LIFE AND CHARGING

To extend the battery life of your Oura Ring, there are several effective strategies you can implement.

Adjust Monitoring Settings: Reduce power consumption by adjusting the heart rate monitoring settings. Opt for periodic monitoring instead of continuous tracking, which can save battery life.

Optimize Sleep Tracking: Enable **Airplane Mode** during sleep to prevent Bluetooth from syncing constantly, conserving battery. This reduces unnecessary power usage while maintaining essential sleep-tracking data.

Bluetooth Management: Disconnect your Oura Ring from Bluetooth when not actively syncing data to avoid additional battery drain.

Charging Practices: Always charge your Oura Ring using the provided cable to ensure the battery lasts longer. Avoid third-party chargers, which may affect the battery performance. As for charging, here's a simple way to effectively charge your ring

Place the Ring on the Charging Dock: Align the ring with the charging dock and ensure it fits securely.

Connect the Dock to a Power Source: Plug the USB cable into a charger or computer. **Check Battery Status in the App**: Open the Oura app on your smartphone to monitor the battery status and confirm it's charging.

CUSTOMIZING YOUR OURA RING

To customize your Oura Ring's app notifications and health reminders, follow these steps:

Customize Notifications:

1. **Open the Oura App**: Start by opening the Oura app on your phone.

2. **Go to Settings**: Tap on your profile icon or navigate to the "Settings" section.

3. **Notification Settings**: Scroll to find "Notifications" or similar options. You can customize the type of alerts you receive for activity, sleep, and other health-related reminders.

4. **Set Preferences**: Toggle the specific alerts, such as movement reminders or sleep notifications, to suit your needs. You can also adjust how often you receive these notifications based on your activity level.

Customizing Health Goals:

1. **Open the Oura App**: Tap on the app to open it.

2. **Access Health Goals**: In the app's main screen, go to the "Health" tab, then navigate to the "Goals" section.

3. **Adjust Goals**: Select the goals you wish to modify, such as steps, exercise duration, or calories burned. You can set daily, weekly, or customized goals.

4. **Personalize Reminders**: Once goals are set, adjust your reminder notifications to prompt you when you're near reaching these goals, or if you're falling behind.

This customization will help you stay aligned with your fitness and health priorities while making the most of Oura's advanced features.

Adjusting personal data

To adjust your activity and sleep targets in the Oura app, follow these steps:

1. **Sleep Preferences**:

   o Open the Oura app and navigate to the **Profile** section.

   o Tap **Sleep Preferences** to adjust the optimal sleep window, such as setting your target bedtime or wake-up time.

   o You can also modify the recommended sleep duration, depending on your individual needs.

2. **Fitness Goals**:

   o To adjust fitness targets, tap the **Activity** card on your home screen.

   o Select **Edit Activity Goal**, where you'll be able to choose either an **Active Calorie Burn** or **Steps** goal. You can use a slider to set the baseline target.

- If you'd prefer not to track calories, enable the **"Calorie opt-out"** option, so only step counts will be shown in the app.

- Oura will adjust your daily activity goal automatically based on your **Readiness Score**. If your score is high, your goal will increase, and if your score is low, it will decrease.

3. **Adjusting Intensity**:

While you can't directly adjust the intensity of your daily goals, Oura does automatically calculate your intensity through the activity type you log. For workouts like running, cycling, or swimming, select the appropriate intensity (e.g., moderate, intense) when logging the activity. The app adjusts these parameters based on the workout's duration and type.

.This approach allows you to personalize your health and fitness goals within the app based on your lifestyle and recovery needs.

TROUBLESHOOTING

To resolve common Oura Ring issues, here are some solutions:

Syncing Issues: Ensure your Oura Ring is within Bluetooth range and connected to your phone. If syncing problems persist, restarting the Oura app or your phone may help. If the connection still fails, consider unpairing the ring and re-pairing it with the app.

Charging or Turning On: If the ring is not charging or turning on, ensure it is placed properly on the charger, and check that the charger is working by testing with another device. Also, confirm the battery level in the app.

Inaccurate Data Readings: Oura Ring can sometimes show inaccurate data due to poor sensor contact or external interference (such as tightness of the ring or movements during sleep). Ensure the ring fits snugly on your finger without being too tight or loose. If data discrepancies continue, a factory reset might help.

Connectivity Issues with Bluetooth: Weak Bluetooth signals or obstructions (like walls) can cause connection problems. Make sure there is a clear path between your phone and the Oura Ring, and check that Bluetooth is enabled on both devices. If that doesn't work, resetting your Oura Ring might resolve persistent issues.

How to contact Oura support

For contacting Oura customer support and accessing helpful resources, here's a guide:

1. **Contacting Oura Support**:

In-App Help Center: Open the Oura app, go to **Settings**, and select **Help**. This will connect you with support options, including FAQs and live chat.

Online Support: Visit the official Oura support website, where you can browse various help topics or start a chat with customer service for direct assistance.

Email Support: If needed, you can email Oura's customer service directly via their official contact page for detailed inquiries.

Maintaining Your Oura Ring

To maintain your Oura Ring effectively, follow these key practices.

Cleaning: Gently clean the ring with mild soap and water, ensuring it's thoroughly rinsed and dried. Avoid abrasive cleaners or chemicals, as they can damage the ring's finish. Regular cleaning prevents the buildup of dirt and oils that can interfere with its sensors.

Preventing Water and Sweat Damage: While the Oura Ring is water-resistant, prolonged exposure to water (e.g., swimming in chlorinated pools or saltwater) and excessive sweat can still impact its durability. Remove the ring during intense water activities if possible.

Scratch Prevention: To reduce scratches, wear your ring on your non-dominant hand, avoid stacking it with other rings, and take it off during activities involving friction (e.g., weightlifting). Avoid rough surfaces and materials like metal or stone that may scratch the ring.

Storage: When not in use, store the Oura Ring in a cool, dry place away from direct sunlight. Excessive heat can damage the battery and electronics, so avoid leaving it in hot environments for extended periods.

These practices will help you extend the ring's lifespan and keep its tracking accurate.

Software Updates How to check for software updates for the Oura Ring Updating the Oura app and firmware for improved features

Software Updates

To keep your Oura Ring running optimally, you should regularly check for software updates on both the Oura app and the ring's firmware. Here's a step-by-step guide on how to do this:

Checking for Software Updates

1. **Oura App Updates**: Go to your device's app store (Google Play Store or Apple App Store) and search for "Oura" to see if an update is available. Regular app updates help maintain compatibility and improve features.

2. **Firmware Updates**:

Open the Oura app on your phone.

If a new firmware update is available, a notification will appear on the app's Home screen.

Tap "Update Now" in the notification message to start the firmware update.

Important: Ensure your Oura Ring has at least a 50% battery level and Bluetooth is enabled on your phone during this process.

For the firmware update to go smoothly, avoid closing the app or toggling Bluetooth off. If the update fails, try restarting your phone, moving to an area with minimal Bluetooth interference, or reinstalling the Oura app. Additionally, always keep your phone's operating system up to date to ensure compatibility with the Oura app and firmware updates.

Quran Ring 4 Vs. Ring 3

The Oura Ring 4 brings several notable upgrades compared to the Oura Ring 3, making it an appealing choice for users interested in enhanced fitness and health tracking. Here's a breakdown of the main differences between the two models:

1. **Design and Comfort**: Both rings are sleek, but the Oura Ring 4 refines this further with an all-titanium design, slightly reduced thickness, and recessed sensors, improving comfort. It also comes in more sizes (4-15) than the Ring 3 (sizes 6-13), which helps in fitting a wider range of users.

2. **Enhanced Sensor Technology**: The Oura Ring 4 includes "Smart Sensing" technology, which combines an expanded sensor array and algorithm improvements. This setup allows for better accuracy in data tracking, particularly for metrics like blood oxygen levels (SpO2), heart rate, and temperature monitoring. The recessed sensors also mean fewer signal interruptions, making the Oura Ring 4 about 30% more accurate in blood oxygen readings than the Gen 3.

3. **Battery Life**: The Oura Ring 4 provides up to 8 days of battery life, slightly more than the Oura Ring 3's 7 days. This added power supports the new advanced tracking features without sacrificing convenience, though both models still require a puck-style charging dock.

4. **New Features**: The Oura Ring 4 introduces automatic activity detection with heart rate tracking, Daytime Stress

insights, and fertility tracking, adding more context to daily habits and stress levels. These improvements make it a better fit for those wanting comprehensive daily wellness insights.

5. **Pricing and Availability**: The Oura Ring 4 starts at $349, with higher-end finishes priced up to $499. Meanwhile, the Oura Ring 3, which has been available since 2021, can be found at discounted prices, though it may be phased out as stocks run low.

Overall, the Oura Ring 4 offers better accuracy and more features, making it a worthwhile upgrade for those who prioritize advanced wellness tracking. However, the Oura Ring 3 remains a strong option for users on a budget.

CONCLUSION

The Oura Ring 4 is a cutting-edge smart ring designed to bring health insights directly to your fingertip with Smart Sensing technology. This adaptive feature customizes readings based on your finger's unique structure, skin tone, and current activity, ensuring highly accurate data while conserving battery life.

A recap of its comprehensive suite of health monitoring and wellness insights, designed to provide users with in-depth understanding and control over their health is as follows :

- Green and infrared PPG sensors provide continuous heart rate monitoring 24/7. They also measure heart rate variability (HRV) and respiration rate during sleep, which are crucial for understanding stress, recovery, and overall heart health.

- An integrated digital temperature sensor measures body temperature variations, giving insights into metabolic health, stress, and even early illness detection.

- A built-in accelerometer tracks your movement and activity all day, helping you stay on top of your physical activity levels.

- Monitors blood oxygen levels during sleep to track respiratory health and detect potential disruptions.

- Assesses cardiovascular health relative to age, giving a personalized measure of heart health.

- Estimates VO2 Max for a measure of aerobic fitness, helping users improve endurance and cardiovascular performance.

- Provides menstrual cycle tracking and insights for

reproductive health.

- Monitors stress levels throughout the day to support stress management.

- Sets and adjusts personalized activity goals based on daily routines and detected activity levels.

- Accesses experimental features and cutting-edge insights in health tracking.

- Uses body temperature and other metrics to support pregnancy-related health monitoring. Tracks recovery and stress management through heart rate variability.

- Offers weekly, monthly, quarterly, yearly, and anniversary reports to monitor long-term trends and progress in wellness.

These features make the Oura Ring 4 a powerful, all-in-one solution for anyone looking to improve and understand their health and wellness.